I Got You an Elephant

For Christmas!

Written and Illustrated

by K.C. Gardner

ISBN-13: 978-1986304818

ISBN-10: 1986304817

Library of Congress
Control Number: 2018904339

This book is dedicated to my dear nephews, and to anyone with a heart for animals.

Acknowledgments:

To my Dad, without your help this book may never have come to fruition. Your knowledge regarding the digital aspect of this process was invaluable. I thank you so much for your tireless efforts to see this project through to completion. Thanks for always being there for me, believing in and encouraging me, and just for being an all-around great Dad. Love You!

To my friend, Ludim Valdez, thanks for always helping with ideas, and letting me know what works and what doesn't. Thanks also for your proofreading skills. I hope you know how helpful you've been and how much I value your friendship.

Dear Reader, this book can be personalized to fit your needs - just fill in the blanks to fit your intended recipients situation. This book can be for a son, daughter, brother, sister, cousin, nephew, friend, etc.

Originally I wrote this for my nephews. At the time one of them was 3, the other 5. This book was written because I had to explain to my 3 year old nephew that I got him an elephant for Christmas, but was not able to bring him over. I thought the best way to explain it to him was by writing this story.

Enjoy!

Dear ___________,

   I got you an elephant for Christmas. I was going
to bring him over today, but here's what happened...
I took Sugar Puppy for a walk.
Mr. Zapenski was walking an elephant.
   "What are you doing with that elephant?" I
asked.
Mr. Zapenski pointed to two men in the distance.
   "See those men? They are bad guys, poachers.

They said they were going to hurt this elephant
and take his ivory tusks. So when they were not
looking, I took him."
  "My house is too small for an elephant, but you
have a big house. Do you want him as a pet?" he
asked. I thought about it for a minute, and said,
"Yes, _________ loves elephants and it's almost
       (child's name)   Christmas."
"What a great gift he'd make!" I said. "Wonderful,"
said Mr. Zapenski. "Now hurry home before the
poachers notice he's gone and come looking."

Mr. Elephant, Sugar Puppy and I quickly trotted home. Mr. Elephant could not squeeze through the front door, so we went through the garage.
  "Uh Oh."
We still had a small door to get through. Mr. Elephant spotted the toolbox, opened a drawer with his trunk, grabbed a hammer, and began knocking down the wall.
  "Mr. Elephant, you are so smart, and your trunk is quite handy," I said.

   Sugar Puppy ran into the house and plopped onto
her favorite chair, so Mr. Elephant and I did all
of the work. Once we got the wall down, Mr.
Elephant played with Sugar Puppy, and I cleaned
up the mess. I was tired and sore, so I filled my
tub with bubble bath. While I was waiting for it
to fill, I started a load of laundry.

Bubbles began to fill the room. Sugar Puppy was barking and chasing bubbles all over the house.

"Where are all the bubbles coming from?" I wondered. Mr. Elephant was blowing bubbles out of his trunk. "Mr. Elephant, you drank my entire bathtub full of bubbles!" I exclaimed. "That's okay Mr. Elephant. You are so big, you probably drink about 40 gallons of water a day.

The tub will be your new water dish.
   I'll take a shower instead," I said.
After my shower, I was hungry, so I went into
the kitchen and.....

"What a Mess!"

There were empty food boxes, Sugar Puppy's nose was in the peanut butter jar, juice was all over the floor, and icky, sticky, gooey slime was all over Mr. Elephant.

"Oh no, more cleaning!"

"Mr. Elephant, you are so big, you probably spend most of your day eating.
     You and Sugar Puppy go outside and play, while I clean up in here," I said.
I finished cleaning up the very messy kitchen, then went outside to check on Mr. Elephant and Sugar Puppy, and...

"Oh no, Mr. Elephant, were you still hungry?"
He ate my grapevine, my acacia tree, and my
flowers!

Mr. Elephant and Sugar Puppy
were rolling in the mud.
"Bath time," I said.

    Mr. Elephant went right to his new water dish,
sucked up all the water with his trunk,
then squirted the water all over himself
and Sugar Puppy.

"Aww, you gave yourself and Sugar Puppy a bath for me. Thanks, Mr. Elephant," I said. I dried them off.
"Bedtime," I said..

Sugar Puppy got in her bed, and Mr. Elephant curled up right next to her. I covered them both and gave them each a kiss good night.

"Finally!" I was looking forward to getting eight hours of sleep. Four hours later, I was awake....

Mr. Elephant was splashing around in his water dish and playing with Sugar Puppy's toys. Sugar Puppy was having fun too, but not me, I was tired, so I went to another room to sleep. I couldn't. I guess elephants don't need as much sleep as people do.

I could hear Mr. Elephant trumpeting and
Sugar Puppy barking and playing.
I got up and turned on the television.

"Breaking news...missing elephant...if found, please call our station."

The poachers tricked the reporters into believing they loved and missed Mr. Elephant, but I knew the truth.

"Oh No!" Mr. Zapenski gave Mr. Elephant to me, and I was going to give him to you. I wasn't sure what to do. Mr. Zapenski had taken the elephant without permission, but only because he was trying to save him.

"Knock, knock."

Mr. Zapenski was at the door with his friend, Amy Bluedeem, a zookeeper.

"Don't worry. I have a plan that should make everyone happy, everyone except the poachers anyway," she said.

Ms. Bluedeem told me all about her zoo. She and the workers there know about elephants and how to care for them. She said elephants enjoy being around other elephants, and they need a lot of room to roam.

    Ms. Bluedeem said that through the zoo's "Adopt an Animal" program, I can still give Mr. Elephant to you. He'll just have to live at the zoo instead of your house.

    Sugar Puppy and I went with Ms. Bluedeem to drop Mr. Elephant off at his new home. He loved it. He was happy to be with other elephants.

    Mr. Elephant can't wait to meet you.

  Ms. Bluedeem said you can come visit your elephant anytime you want!
  After we dropped Mr. Elephant off, Sugar Puppy was sad.
  She missed having a friend to play with, but I told her not to worry because...

I got your ________________,________________

a giraffe for christmas!

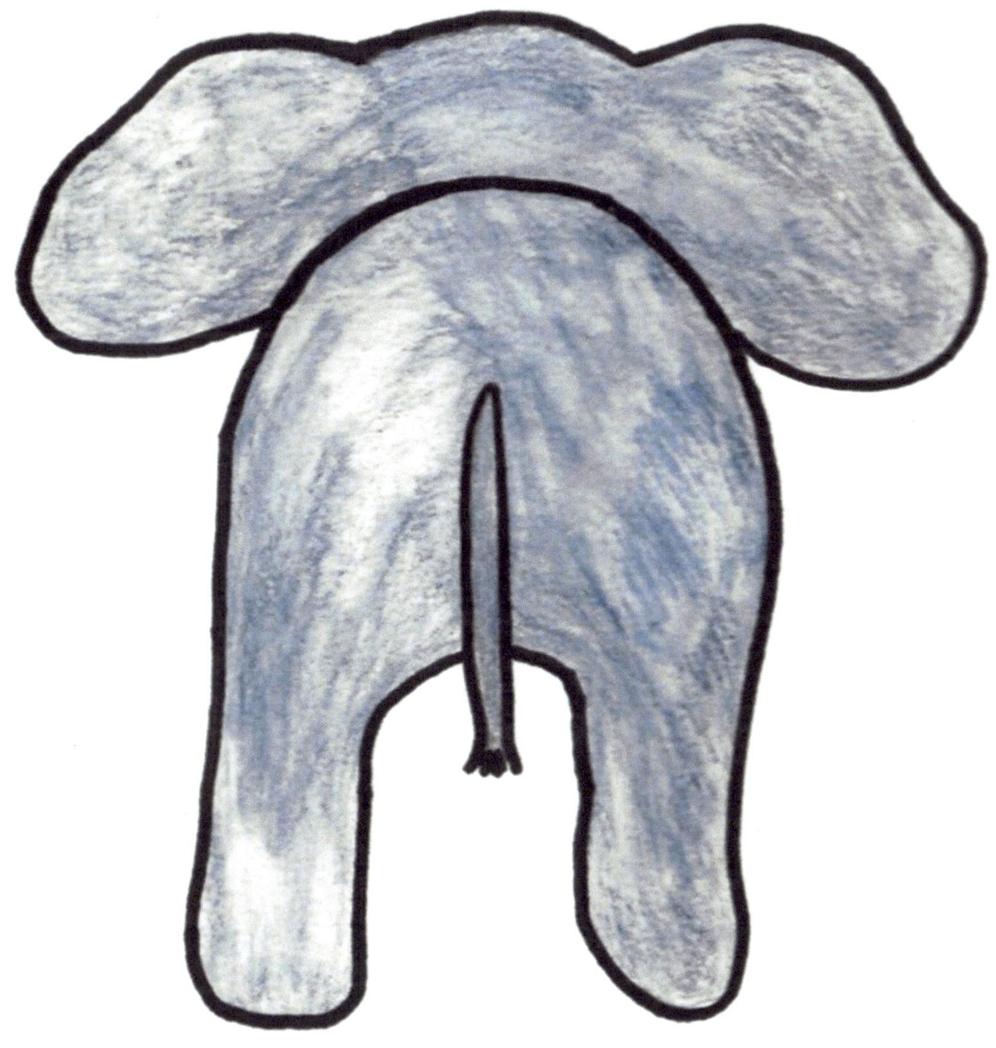

The End

About the Author

K.C. Gardner resides in southern California with her dog, Sugar Puppy. She is the doting aunt of 3 young nephews, and she would save every animal in the world, if she could.

K.C. has worked as a preschool teacher for the majority of her adult life, and is sometimes referred to as "the biggest kid on the playground!" If her co-workers were to read this, they would most likely say, "What do you mean sometimes?"

K.C.'s interests are varied, to the point that it is amazing she was able to stay focused long enough to actually get this book written and out into the world.

K.C.'s varied interests include photography, sketching, writing, painting, roller skating, running, and gymnastics.

I am sure that she will be writing more children's books, and hopefully soon.

I should know, as I am her Dad and I could not be more proud of her.

Michael J. Gardner

www.ingramcontent.com/pod-product-compliance
Lightning Source LLC
Chambersburg PA
CBHW040039240726
48664CB00003B/988